A Bee Story

by Prophet Kervin Dieudonne

Contents

<u>**Introduction**</u>

In the beginning God created the Heavens and the Earth. The world was void and darkness was over the face of the deep. There was no creation. It was merely a big empty space. But in the midst of it, there was a God who called himself by many names. He is to be the Alpha and Omega. He is to be the first and the last. He is to be the beginning and the end. He spoke of His birth to be from everlasting to everlasting. There is none above Him and no one can ever be like Him. From himself, He had a family that is through Him and this family is composed of three characters called the Holy Trinity. The Trinity is composed of the Father, the Son, and the Holy Spirit. What makes God beautiful is the Trinity. It is what makes Him God. It is who He is. It's His nature. The three are inseparable. They are One within themselves and powerful in nature. He lives in a world called the spiritual world. In the beginning there was only the spiritual world. Thus, His kingdom and palace are in the spiritual world.

His wisdom and understanding continually surpass our imagination and understanding. In the beginning, the God from everlasting to everlasting saw the need for creation. All by himself, He created the Heavens and the Earth. He created one everlasting out of the existence of eternity. He sent the Holy Spirit to look over the face of the deep and observe what needed to be done as signs of creation. It is written in Genesis Chapter 1:1-3, ***"In the beginning God created the Heavens and the earth. Now the earth was formless and empty, darkness was over the surface of the deep, and the Spirit of God was hovering over the waters. And God said, "Let there be light," and there was light.""*** The Holy Spirit went to and fro between the heavens and the Earth, searching for what needed to be created and what needed to be made. Such marvelous ideas He had! What beautiful things He envisioned. He was so filled with ideas that, when He returned home to the Father and the Son, He began explaining to them what could be done and they loved it. It was so exciting. God spoke and said, *"Let there be light"* and the light appeared. From that point on they began to see things clearly. All that the Holy Spirit envisioned was created. Everything we see, He created. Those are His ideas: the trees, sun, moon and the stars, the waters, air, food, living creatures, those that can fly, walk, swim in waters, creatures that crawl or hop, all different kinds of creatures. He breathed life into all of them and they became living creatures. Something new was created every day and it took Him seven days in our time to create everything. The interesting part of this story is, on the fifth day, God created creatures that are called animals. They were made to live in a place called nature. On the sixth day He said, "I want to create something that looks like Me," and He created what is called a human being. He gave him a name. He called him Adam. Adam was very lucky because out of all God's creations only Adam looked like Him. God created a home for Adam and He called the place Eden. A garden out of God's amazing creations, Eden was quite exquisite. It was filled with many different types of fruits, trees, rivers, and streams. It was almost like a glimpse of God's own house because He wanted man to live freely and to be like Him, created in His image. Now, there was one particular tree that was in Eden that God told Adam not to touch or eat from. In every house there is a secret box that your parents do not want you to go into. Well, it was the same for Adam since God was His creator. God had a secret box (tree) in the garden and He told Adam not to touch it. God had a specific name for this tree. He called it the tree of the knowledge of evil and good. With such a name, I can see why God kept it a secret as well as why He didn't want Adam to touch it. But let's continue with the story.

God had other servants in His house that were working for Him. He calls them angels. Although there were many angels, He had one in particular that was very close to Him. His name was Lucifer. Lucifer was so close to God that he was put in charge of many things in Gods house. Lucifer was built in beauty. He was the morning star and he was almost at the age of perfection. Lucifer had other angels who were under him and working for him. But Lucifer had a problem. Pride was found in him because he wanted to be like God although he was not created to be in the image or likeness of God. Therefore, Lucifer, in his pride, began to grow in jealousy. He was cast out of Heaven along with the angels who followed him in rebellion. He sought to destroy man and disconnect man from God. God had already given Adam a wife at that time and she was named Eve. Lucifer decided to use the one tree that God had forbidden man to eat from. The Lord spoke to Adam and told him not to eat from the tree of the knowledge of evil and good and that's where Lucifer convinced man to disobey God. He went against the Word of God concerning what God said to Adam. It was that tree that Lucifer used to convince Adam to disobey God. Lucifer went to the garden to put Adam in confusion. Lucifer lied to Adam and told him that he would not die, but rather, he would be able to see in the same manner as God. The Bible says Lucifer was so convincing. Eve came and took from the tree. She ate and afterward she gave it to Adam who ate as well. From that time on, man begin to see a lot of things God did not want them to see. They opened the secret box and they began to know the secrets that they should not have known. God felt pained and He was hurt because He wanted man to be His friend. But they disobeyed Him so He had to make a decision. God spoke to His family and disappointedly said man has become like us, therefore they cannot stay in the Garden of Eden anymore. There was another tree in the Garden called the tree of life. It was a tree that could allow them to live for eternity just like God. So God said I cannot allow them to eat from the tree of life. I can't allow them to live in the garden anymore. They cannot have access to the tree of life. I have to kick them out. God kicked man out and from there man was on his own. Communication with God was cut off. Adam and Eve began to struggle. Even the simple act of living was hard for them.

Man had a new friend and he was called sin. Sin was not kind like God was to them. Sin was rather rude and abusive toward the man called Adam. Sin started killing every beautiful thing that was created by God. Sin even crippled Adam's destiny and descendants. Sin knew neither mercy nor compassion. Sin made them live a hard life and even made them do things they had never seen God do. Those things started to destroy them. Sin started to make its own creations through man. But sin's creations were wicked and very destructive. Sin had power and controlled the life of man. From there on, it was very sad in the eyes of God and His family when they looked at what sin did to their creation. Sadly, God said He regretted that He made man. He regretted how He created man to look like Him and He came to a decision to destroy everything that they had made. But there was one man that looked like His Son and his name was Noah. It was because of Noah that everything was not destroyed. God said because Noah resembled His Son, He would not bring everything to complete destruction. Although God planned to destroy everything, he would let Noah, his family, and two of every kind of every creature survive the destruction of His wrath. God then called Noah and commanded him to build an ark because He was going to destroy everything with a flood. Noah was to get his family along with two of every kind of animal and place them in the ark so that they may survive the flood that was going to come. Noah obeyed the Lord and followed His instructions just as the Lord directed. It is from the ark and the story of Adam that the "Man versus Bee Nature" was seen. Noah had all these different types of animals in the ark, but there was one particular creation that is called the "Bee" and the story begins from there.

The Holy Spirit begins to tell His side of the story.

A Story That Will Change Your Life

The Holy Spirit is one of the family members of the Trinity. With a sad heart, He begins to tell His story after the great flood. When the Father destroyed humanity and everything along with it except for Noah, his family, and two of every kind of animal, after Noah came out of the ark by observation of a certain flying creature called the "Bee," the Holy Spirit begins to explain His story in parables through Mr. Bee...

It was centuries ago, ages before the great Son of Man called Jesus Christ, The Anointed One, came from the Father. The world was in great trials because of sin and I saw a flying creature that speaks of what happened to the paradise that God had created. The creature is named Bee-Nature. It is a small creature, a two winged flying insect with a stinger as a tail. Mr. Bee feeds on nectar and pollen, and produces honey and beeswax. He has a family that is composed of 20,000 members called a colony. As I was watching this creature working among its colony collecting nectar to produce its honey, it reminded me of the man called sin. I watched Mr. Bee wake up every day and go into the field to collect the nectar in order to produce the honey. That is when I saw the man called Adam. He was like a flower in the eyes of God. His aroma in the nose of God was a smell that filled Him with Glory of perfection that His work was perfect in His eyes. Adam was like a beautiful garden in the eyes of God, the perfect resemblance of His image to represent Him on earth as He is in Heaven. But Adam was getting sucked dry. He was losing the perfect gifts that God had placed in him. Even the sweet smell and pleasing aroma to God was beginning to vanish. Adam was not only losing his strength, but even the anointing that was upon his life was leaving because Mr. Bee was sucking him dry every day. I then looked at Mr. Bee and I said, "Who are you representing?" Instantly, it reminded me of the tempter who is called by the name of Lucifer. It reminded me of how he stole God's creation by taking it from Adam after creation was given to Adam for him to rule over. It reminded me of Lucifer, his legion, and his whole family of agents that have come to tempt mankind. I saw Mr. Bee in his resemblance. Mr. Bee was an agent working and sucking Gods creations dry. Mr. Bee was there to suck out the destiny that had been placed in man. Mr. Bee represents the friend Adam had called sin. That's when it all made sense. It was becoming clear to me by the Holy Spirit, through the story He was telling me as I was meditating on His Word.

Sin produced many characters and had become a default in the life of man to destroy the good and perfect will of God. I began to see the pattern of Mr. Bee, and how he could be a representation of any default in our lives. Mr. Bee could be a spirit of jealousy that is in our lives to torment us, to sting our destiny and stop us from seeing the glory of God. Mr. Bee could be anything that we do that is not pleasing to God, or anything that has to do with disobeying the good and perfect will of God. It is Mr. Bee that is in sin's likeness, just as the Bible says it comes to kill, to steal, and to destroy. That is his work. It is his mission to do acts against the will of God. To understand this story, first understand that Mr. Bee represents sin. Every day, sin stings us in order to stop us from the will of God. The thing is that it is a slow death because one Bee cannot destroy a man. It has to be many of them, hundreds even. Mr. Bee comes every day and takes the goodness of God out of men and leaves them for dead. This reminds me of the story in Ezekiel 37, how Ezekiel saw the dry bones in the desert and the Lord God asked him, are they able to live again? Literally they were not really dead bones that Ezekiel saw, rather the Lord was showing him people who looked like dead bones. How they had no life or energy in them, because Mr. Bee had sucked them dry. The Lord had to declare to Ezekiel that they were indeed able to live again. Mr. Bee is not a good friend of man because when he comes, he will suck you dry and there is nothing good that can come out of that.

According to the story of the Holy Spirit, God has placed His goodness in mankind that can produce honey and that is the reason why Mr. Bee has an attraction to us. The pollen that it feeds on and uses to produce its honey could be represented as the goodness of God in our lives, our destiny that will bring forth our blessings. Because of your destiny, sin will come to cripple your life because of what God wants you to do. Sin comes to destroy you and that is the same thing the story is trying to reveal me according to the explanation of the Holy

Spirit. Mr. Bee wants to take everything for himself in order to produce its own honey, and that is when I understood it. Sin takes from us and brings it to its kind. Mr. Bee has a home that is called the nest, and in its nest are thousands of Bees. They are all working against the goodness of God. They are very alert and have very protective personal security called the "sting." That's when I grasped the meaning of the Scripture when Paul said, *"the sting of death is sin."* If the tempter wants to kill you, he has to first get you to sin. It is a patient and slow death, but it will get the job done. Let's go back to this nest we are talking about. It is a representation of the world. All of the money that is in the world, all the riches, major houses, millionaires, and billionaires- 90 percent of them are in the world. Just as a bee leaves the nest to feed on flowers and produce the honey, in the same manner, sin feeds on the destiny of men. Sin steals men's glory and transforms it into darkness and wickedness. This wickedness is the abomination of sin portraying the goodness and the blessings of God: such as lies, ambition, jealousy, hatred, pride and murder. Sin uses these things to make people wealthy. It takes the goodness of God in us and uses it to produces the honey of its own. In that same manner, the tempter is stealing from the children of God to give to his children. Jesus said Satan is their father, for he is the father of lies. This is the only Scripture that is in the Bible that addresses Satan as the father of lies. That means he is the one who invented lies. God did not create lies, the tempter did. Satan lies to us and steals what we have been given from God to give to his own followers. If someone is a father, it means that there must be children who belong to him.

Thus, the tempter steals our nectar and produces honey for his children. Look at what he did to Adam. Adam was kicked out of the Garden and allowed Lucifer to gain control of the world. In Luke 4, he offered the world to Jesus because he was the one who had possession of it. The honey in the nest already belongs to you. But you need to overcome Mr. Bee in order to take it back from him. The tempter has to steal from you because he has nothing of his own to give except lies. He takes from you in order to give to his children. Sin has the power to rob you of your gift and in turn make you work for the tempter so the good will of God is not fulfilled in you. What's in the nest is already yours and you must take it back. You have all your rights to eat it as much as you please because it was already yours to begin with. The tempter has clouded your knowledge, for the Scriptures say, *"lack of knowledge my people are perishing."* He clouds your knowledge and understanding so you don't see yourself. He has lied to you and introduced you to Sin, so that you can live a life that he wants you to live. The Holy Spirit then showed me that it is very ironic how the bee that Stings is the very same bee that produces honey. In other words, remember that the Bee represents sin, the sin that clouds your life. You need to walk through in order to reclaim your destiny. If you have a sin in your life that is tormenting you, you must conquer it so that you can win your victory. Just think for a moment. Why are millionaires committing suicide? People that reach a high level in life are killing themselves. Why? Because they never did win a true victory over their "sin." They were still being controlled by their sin and the tempter was leading them. You have to go into the nest to take back what is yours. The Bible says that before Israel left Egypt, the Lord God commanded them to go to the Egyptian's houses to ask them for gold and anything else that they wanted from them. Egypt was the nest and it was in Egypt where the riches were. God told them not to leave Egypt without claiming their possessions from there. The best thing about it is they had worked for it. For 400 years they were held in bondage and slavery. The tempter knows how to steal from you and only the Lord can remove the cloud to make you see clearly His good and perfect will. Don't be afraid to go into the nest and take back what belongs to you.

I'm going to explain to you how we have the power to go into the nest because what's in the nest is yours. God did not make you to live in poverty. That is the lie of the tempter. God did not create you to be sick. That is the lie of the tempter. God did not make you to look like Him and to live in sin. That's the lie of the tempter! Whatever God is, that is who you are; His likeness, His image. You were made to be like Him! In the Book of John Chapter 10 Jesus said, *"Isn't written that you yourself is call gods,"* that is why He is the King of kings and He is the Lord of lords. Because you were not only made to be like Him but to also have power, dominion, and authority! Hallelujah! You must go into the nest and claim what is yours! Amen.

The Way To Victory Over Sin

It was in the years AD, from the creation of Adam to the great flood, from Noah to Abraham, from Abraham to Joseph, from Joseph to Moses, from Moses to David, from David to Solomon, from Solomon establishing the kingdom of David by the Word and the promise of God. God sent one member of His family to help mankind get back closer to Him. Just like the Scriptures say, *"For God so love the world He gave His only begotten Son whosoever believes in Him shall not perish but have eternal life."* (John 3:16) The Bible says, with His own mouth the Son of God stated that all those who came after Him would be thieves, and they would not be the door to Heaven. But He *is* the door to heaven. Surprisingly, the Son of God was born out of a woman because God wanted Him to be 100 percent human so He could help human kind. His birth was supernatural. His mother was a virgin named Mary. Or, should I say Mary was only there to carry Him, but His real mother is the Holy Spirit. The Scriptures say Mary was a young virgin that was destined to be married to a man named Joseph. Before the marriage could happen however, Mary got pregnant without even laying with Joseph. Joseph started to doubt Mary, thinking that she did something behind his back. He even thought that she committed adultery. According to the law, she would have to be stoned to death. The Bible says that while Joseph was in distress, he fell into a sleep and an angel of the Lord came and spoke to him. The angel said that the child in the womb of Mary was the Savior of the world. The child was the work of God through Mary. Joseph believed. He took Mary as his bride and Jesus came to be born.

From His birth to the age of 12, Jesus began doing the work of the Father. It was important to Jesus to do the Father's work, seeing how much man was struggling because of sin. He was mankind's last hope of reconciliation back to the Father. If Jesus failed the mission, then all of mankind would have been annihilated. He was focused on doing the will of the Father, right from the start, fasting for 40 days and fighting against wild beasts. From there He was tempted by the devil. Just as he had tempted Adam and Eve, the tempter attacked Jesus as well. But He rebuked him by saying, *"You shall not tempt the Lord your God."* Jesus starting preaching and teaching how to reconcile with God. He stated His nature in God, that He *is* the *way*, the *truth* and the *life*. He showed them great miracles, signs, and wonders, although it was still hard for many to perceive Him as who He said He was. Jesus never stopped preaching, being a member of the Holy Trinity family. He saw from the very beginning how man struggled because of sin. He saw what they went through from losing their relationship with the Father. So He came to help them. Man was killing his own kind without the Father's guidance. Now imagine that the person who made you ended up abandoning you without giving you the knowledge or understanding of your existence. It was hard to survive without fellowship with the Father. He felt man's pain and that's why He came down on a mission.

That mission was to bring man back to the Father. He was not going to stop until the mission was fulfilled, even if it meant He had to die. That is why in the Scriptures, He bore our sin and iniquities on His back. He carried our transgressions just so we could be closer to the Father. The Scriptures say, in Jesus we come to know creation and everything old passes away. Everything else becomes new. Only in Him can we receive true life from the grip and power of sin. Sin messed us up. Christ had to deal with our infirmities and demons, our wickedness. Sin closed the heart of man because we did not have the guidance of the Father. Imagine being raised without a father or mother. You would grow up to do whatever you please. You would not understand truth, love, nor kindness. It was the same way with us. Man was raised without a Father. Jesus saw it, and we suffered because of it. He wanted to make us know God as our Father. Understand this: without Christ, God is only our Creator. But with the acceptance of Christ, we are able to know God as our Father. When He is our Creator, He feels hurt, disappointed, or may even want to destroy us. When He is a Father, He is more compassionate and loving toward us. Because of Christ, God has to accept us and loves us. Therefore, anyone who denies Jesus is a fool because they have to deal with the Creator, with no promise of mercy or grace. The Scriptures say, because of Jesus, we do not have a spirit of slaves or bondage anymore but we have a spirit of sonship that lets us cry *"Abba Father."* Jesus gives you access to call the Father, "Daddy." Imagine when you get to Heaven. You don't have to worship or love Him as Creator, but you worship and love Him as Father. Jesus gives you that access when you accept Him. It is in Him that there is truth and light. Sin has its contract. It is a contract of suffering to slowly kill you or even damn you for eternity. But God has mercy through His son Jesus Christ. We must accept His teachings and His ways because that is what will bring us closer to the Father. Imagine being created and having no knowledge of creation and even your own purpose, Jesus broke that, He is opening the door for you to know who you are and your purpose in the Father. Sin works in packs. One sin attracts every sin. But imagine you have the power to fight against it through the Son of God. I'm talking about total freedom living a life of happiness, living a life free of worry, and trusting in His Son Jesus. Sin is not a true blessing. It will keep blessings away from you. Sin stole them from you, and he will continue to take it away from you to give it to someone else. The Scriptures say, *"God is not a man that he should lie nor the son of Man that he should change his mind."* When Jesus promises you, you better believe it will be established. But you have got to hold on to Him.

The Honey of Your Life

May the honey of this book change your life, in the name of Jesus!

Every sting of sin against you, may it produce 100 times more honey in your life, in the name of Jesus!

The honey stolen from you a long time ago, may it return in the name of Jesus!

The honey that they took to their hives, may it return in the name of Jesus!

The honey of your finances, may it return in the name of Jesus!

The honey of marriage, may it return in the name of Jesus!

The honey of destiny, may it return in the name of Jesus!

The honey of childhood, may it return in the name of Jesus!

The honey of your gift, may it return in the name of Jesus!

The honey that gives your life taste, may it return in the name of Jesus!

The honey of your teenage years, may it return in the name of Jesus!

The honey of your womb, may it return in the name of Jesus!

The honey of your adult years, may it return in the name of Jesus!

17

It Belongs to You

Every voodoo priest who stole your honey; take it back, in the name of Jesus!
Every witch that stole your honey; take it back, in the name of Jesus!
Every witchcraft that pollutes your honey; may it come out now, in the name of Jesus!
Every witch that sucked your honey dry; may they vomit it now, in the name of Jesus!
Every power that stole your belongings; take them back, in the name of Jesus!
Every devil that stole your dreams; take them back, in the name of Jesus!
Every demon that stole your vision; take it back, in the name of Jesus!
Every wicked power that steals your potential; take it back, in the name of Jesus!

Your Taste Shall Return

Let the honeyed flavor of your millions of dollars
return now, in the name of Jesus!
Whatever is for your destiny, receive it now by fire, in
the name of Jesus!
The house of your taste, receive it now, in the name
of Jesus!
The car of your taste, receive it now, in the name of
Jesus!
The job of your taste, receive it now, in the name of
Jesus!
Let your life be filled with honey from the Holy Spirit
to the brim, in the name of Jesus!
The husband of your taste, receive him in the name
of Jesus!
The wife of your taste, receive her in the name of
Jesus!
The business of your taste, receive it in the name of
Jesus!
The land of your taste, receive it in the name of
Jesus!
The blessing of your taste, receive it now, in the name
of Jesus!

Bee Must Be Gone

Let every bee of a generational curse die now, in the name of Jesus.

Let every bee of a curse die now, in the name of Jesus.

Let every bee of voodoo die now, in the name of Jesus.

Let every bee of rumors die now, in the name of Jesus.

Let every bee of accusers die now, in the name of Jesus.

Every bee in my life must die now, in the name of Jesus.

Let every bee of rebellion die now, in the name of Jesus.

Let every bee of gossip die now, in the name of Jesus.

Let every bee of poverty die now, in the name of Jesus.

Let every bee of resistance die now, in the name of Jesus.

Let every bee of witches die now, in the name of Jesus.

Let every bee of pride die now, in the name of Jesus.

Let every bee of negative words, hexes and jinxes die now, in the name of Jesus.

Let every bee of conspiracy die, in the name of Jesus.

Prophet Kervin Dieudonne

Let every bee of enchantment die, in the name of
Jesus.
Let every bee of failure die, in the name of Jesus.
Let every bee of rejection die, in the name of Jesus.

Locate You Now

Anyone with a tongue of a bee that spoke against me,
I destroy in the name of Jesus.
May the billionaire with honey locate me now, in
Jesus' name.
May the prophet with a mouth of honey locate me
now, in Jesus' name.
You, my divine helpers with honey; locate me now in
Jesus' name.
The person that is supposed to bless me with honey;
locate me now, in Jesus' name.
My full potential, locate me in Jesus' name.
My divine destiny, locate me in Jesus' name.
The fullness of my gifts, locate me in Jesus' name.
May my destiny be filled with honey, in Jesus' name.
May my life be filled with honey, in Jesus' name.
May the job I need locate me now, in the name of
Jesus.

<u>About the Author</u>

Prophet Kervin Dieudonne flows in the anointing of teaching, healing, deliverance, and prophecy. The General Overseer of The Worldwide Kingdom Ministry Inc. located in South FL, Prophet Dieudonne is married to the lovely Psalmist Melissa Dieudonne. Together they are determined to advance the body of Christ and have traveled to the majority of Florida, New York, Trinidad, Haiti, Bahamas, Georgia, and other places preaching the good news to the lost, proclaiming freedom for the captives, and releasing prisoners from darkness. Prophet Kervin Dieudonne is the author of "The Prophetic Zone of War," "Servanthood," and "A Preacher's Guide."

Made in the USA
Columbia, SC
10 November 2024

45861815R00020